EXPLORING COUNTRIES
Nepal

by Lisa Owings

BELLWETHER MEDIA • MINNEAPOLIS, MN

Note to Librarians, Teachers, and Parents:

Blastoff! Readers are carefully developed by literacy experts and combine standards-based content with developmentally appropriate text.

Level 1 provides the most support through repetition of high-frequency words, light text, predictable sentence patterns, and strong visual support.

Level 2 offers early readers a bit more challenge through varied simple sentences, increased text load, and less repetition of high-frequency words.

Level 3 advances early-fluent readers toward fluency through increased text and concept load, less reliance on visuals, longer sentences, and more literary language.

Level 4 builds reading stamina by providing more text per page, increased use of punctuation, greater variation in sentence patterns, and increasingly challenging vocabulary.

Level 5 encourages children to move from "learning to read" to "reading to learn" by providing even more text, varied writing styles, and less familiar topics.

Whichever book is right for your reader, Blastoff! Readers are the perfect books to build confidence and encourage a love of reading that will last a lifetime!

This edition first published in 2014 by Bellwether Media, Inc.

No part of this publication may be reproduced in whole or in part without written permission of the publisher. For information regarding permission, write to Bellwether Media, Inc., Attention: Permissions Department, 5357 Penn Avenue South, Minneapolis, MN 55419.

Library of Congress Cataloging-in-Publication Data

Owings, Lisa.
 Nepal / by Lisa Owings.
   pages cm. – (Blastoff! Readers: Exploring Countries)
 Summary: "Developed by literacy experts for students in grades three through seven, this book introduces young readers to the geography and culture of Nepal"– Provided by publisher.
 Includes bibliographical references and index.
 ISBN 978-1-62617-069-8 (hardcover : alk. paper)
 1. Nepal–Juvenile literature. I. Title.
 DS493.4.O95 2014
 954.96–dc23

2013034781

Text copyright © 2014 by Bellwether Media, Inc. BLASTOFF! READERS and associated logos are trademarks and/or registered trademarks of Bellwether Media, Inc. SCHOLASTIC, CHILDREN'S PRESS, and associated logos are trademarks and/or registered trademarks of Scholastic Inc.

Printed in the United States of America, North Mankato, MN.

Contents

Where Is Nepal?	4
The Land	6
Mount Everest	8
Wildlife	10
The People	12
Daily Life	14
Going to School	16
Working	18
Playing	20
Food	22
Holidays	24
The Sherpas of Nepal	26
Fast Facts	28
Glossary	30
To Learn More	31
Index	32

Where Is Nepal?

India

The small country of Nepal covers 56,827 square miles (147,181 square kilometers) in southern Asia. It is sandwiched between two of the largest countries in the world. India surrounds Nepal to the west, south, and east. Across the Himalayan Mountains to the north lies China. The region of China that borders Nepal is called Tibet.

Nepal is completely **landlocked**. With no nearby seas, rivers are its main bodies of water. Flowing south from the Himalayas are the major Karnali, Narayani, and Kosi Rivers. The capital city of Kathmandu stands near the meeting place of the Baghmati and Vishnumati Rivers. It is also the largest city in Nepal.

The Land

Did you know?
The Himalayas are the highest mountain range on Earth. Several of the world's highest peaks lie in Nepal.

Nepal's landscape climbs from the southern lowlands to the snow-capped Himalayas. The flat land along the Indian border is called the Tarai. Streams crisscross the **marshes** here. Rice crops and green forests prosper in the area's **fertile** soil and hot, damp weather. The Tarai rises into the hilly Churia Range.

fun fact

In Nepal, the temperature drops as the mountain peaks climb. Temperatures never rise above freezing in places above 16,000 feet (4,900 meters).

North of the Churia Range, the land dips slightly before continuing upward into the mountains. Many of the mountains in central Nepal are **terraced** with farms. The mighty Himalayas tower over northern Nepal. Many of their frosty peaks loom more than 25,000 feet (7,620 meters) above the lowlands.

Mount Everest

Did you know?
Mount Everest looks solid and still. However, it actually moves northeast a few inches and grows a tiny bit taller each year!

The **summit** of Mount Everest pierces through the clouds along Nepal's northern border. At 29,035 feet (8,850 meters), it is the highest point on Earth. Everest's slopes are steep and unforgiving. Jagged cliffs surround frozen **glaciers** full of deep **crevasses**. Rock and ice are swept downward by deadly **avalanches**. Fierce winds blow streams of snow off Everest's peak.

Climbers from all over the world try to scale Mount Everest. They face a challenging journey. Breathing is a struggle because there is so little oxygen that high up. Climbers also risk falling or being caught in a raging snowstorm. Many climbers die or turn back before they reach the summit. The few who make it get to stand on top of the world.

fun fact
The Sherpa people who live around Everest believe a monster called the yeti, or abominable snowman, wanders its slopes.

Wildlife

tahr

Nepal's warm forests and snowy mountains shelter wildlife of all kinds. In the Tarai, several species of deer run from spotted leopards and Bengal tigers. Asian elephants and the rare Indian rhinoceros can also be found in these lowlands. Storks and cranes comb the marshes for food. Rivers are home to hungry crocodiles and the **endangered** river dolphin.

Bengal tiger

red panda

Indian roller

fun fact

Spotting an Indian roller is considered good luck in Nepal. This bird's bright turquoise wings are hard to miss.

In the hills, Himalayan black bears roam, and barking deer sound their calls. Monkeys often wander into cities looking for scraps. Brightly colored pheasants strut along the slopes. Higher in the mountains are blue sheep and long-haired mountain goats called *tahr*. Red pandas hide in mountain forests. The rarely seen snow leopard comes out at night to hunt.

The People

More than 30 million people live in Nepal. Most of them have **ancestors** from northern India. Others have ancestors who moved south from Tibet. Many Nepali come from mixed backgrounds. About half the county's people speak the official language of Nepali as their first language. Others speak a variety of **native** languages. Most Nepali follow the Hindu religion. Some Tibetan peoples are Buddhist. Hindus and Buddhists often share places of worship.

A **caste** system separates Nepali into different ranks in society. Indian Hindu peoples belong to the highest and lowest social castes. People of other backgrounds belong to the middle castes. Nepali often marry, choose jobs, and interact with others based on their caste. A few Nepali groups live outside the caste system.

Speak Nepali!

Nepali is written in script. However, Nepali words can be written in English to help you read them out loud.

English	Nepali	How to say it
hello	namaste	nah-MAH-stay
good-bye	namaste	nah-MAH-stay
yes	hajur	HAH-jur
no	chhaina	chai-NAH
please	kripaya	kree-PIE-yah
thank you	dhanyabad	DHAN-nai-bat
friend	saathi	SAH-thee

Daily Life

Did you know?
Many marriages in Nepal are arranged by the parents of the couple. The engagement period gives the couple time to decide whether to accept or reject the marriage.

Most people in Nepal live in villages in the countryside. About half build homes of mud or stone on the Tarai. Others carve out land on mountain slopes. Families usually grow their own food and trade any extra for other goods. In the Himalayas, many people rely on **yak** herds. Most Nepali cannot afford cars. They walk or ride bicycles from place to place.

Kathmandu is the only major city in Nepal, although there are several large towns. Buses and taxis help city dwellers travel easily. Nepali in the city live in homes or small apartments. A room is often set aside for Hindu or Buddhist **shrines**.

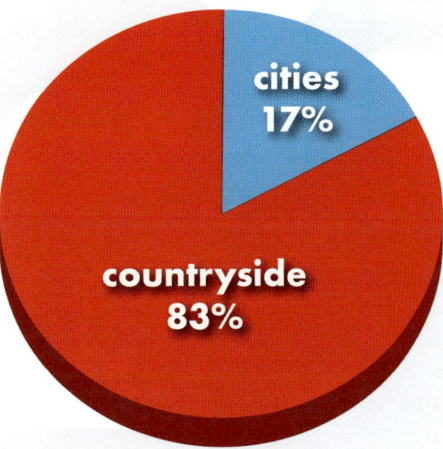

Where People Live in Nepal

cities 17%
countryside 83%

fun fact

Some Nepali believe that much of what happens in life is the will of their gods. Many make offerings to the gods each day in a ritual called *puja*.

Going to School

16

Most Nepali children begin school at age 5. They often have to walk for many miles to get to class. School is free, but families have to work hard to pay for books and supplies. Primary school lasts for five years. Students learn to read and write in Nepali and English. Classes also focus on math and science.

Many students move on to secondary school. Girls are often kept at home to help with chores or to earn extra money for the family. At the end of tenth grade, students take an exam. Those who pass can continue through grade twelve. Secondary school graduates can either take a job or apply to universities.

fun fact

Nepal is working to improve its education system. The government wants to extend primary school through grade eight and help more students stay in school through grade twelve.

Working

Did you know?
Many Nepali cannot find jobs in the country. Some travel across the border to India to find work. They send money home to their families in Nepal.

Where People Work in Nepal

- services 18%
- manufacturing 7%
- farming 75%

fun fact

A number of Tibetans living in Nepal craft beautiful carpets with creative designs. These carpets are sold worldwide and are an important source of income for Nepal.

About three out of every four Nepali work on farms. Some grow rice, corn, potatoes, or sugarcane. Others raise cattle or water buffalo. Most farmers produce only enough food to feed their families. Workers cut down trees in Nepal's forests. Most of the wood is shipped to India. A few mines in the country yield coal, copper, and iron.

Most factory workers make food products. Others produce cloth, bricks, or cement. People who have **service jobs** work in schools and shops. Some have jobs in the hotels and restaurants of Kathmandu. They mainly serve **tourists** and wealthy Nepali.

Playing

When Nepali have free time, they like to spend it with family and friends. Badminton and soccer are favorite sports. Children often make soccer balls with whatever materials they can find. *Kabaddi* is a **traditional** team sport. Players try to wrestle or tag their opponents while they hold their breath. They chant "kabaddi" to prove they are not breathing in.

Groups of friends get together to fly kites. Other favorite activities include playing board games or going for a swim. In cities, many Nepali enjoy going to movies. Some families gather around televisions or radios in the evenings. Local festivals offer music, dancing, and a chance to catch up with friends from other villages.

fun fact

Carroms is a popular board game in Nepal. Similar to pool, players try to flick disks into holes in the corners of the board.

Food

Nepali meals consist mostly of rice and vegetables. The most common meal throughout the country is *daal bhaat*, a spiced lentil soup with rice. This dish is often served with *tarkari*, or curried vegetables. Nepali pour the soup and vegetables onto the rice, then scoop the rice into their mouths with the right hand. *Masu*, or meat, is a rare treat. Water buffalo and goat meat are popular. Hindu Nepali do not eat beef.

Indian flatbreads are often served with meals. Pastries filled with spicy potatoes make delicious snacks. Nepali also enjoy fried dough crisps or spiced peanuts. Sweets include milky fudge called *burfi* and fried orange swirls of *jalebi*. Many Nepali drink hot tea throughout the day.

fun fact

Most places in Nepal serve *chiya*, a hot spiced tea brewed in sweetened milk. In the Himalayas, black tea is flavored with salt and yak butter.

chiya

jalebi

Holidays

Nepali gather for festivals and holidays throughout the year. *Dashain* is the biggest holiday in Nepal. It celebrates the victory of good over evil in life. Schools and businesses shut down for 15 days each fall for the festival. The five-day celebration of *Tihar* comes soon after *Dashain*. On the third evening, Nepali light candles and lamps in their homes to honor the goddess of wealth.

fun fact

May 29 is Republic Day in Nepal. It celebrates the day in 2008 when Nepal came to be ruled by the people instead of by royalty.

Republic Day

Did you know?
Nepali have a blast splashing each other with water and colorful powders during the festival of *Holi*. Visitors are their favorite targets!

The Nepali New Year starts in mid-April. The festival of *Bisket Jatra* kicks off the celebrations. Crowds of Nepali haul **chariots** through the streets to the sound of traditional music. In the spring, Buddha's birthday is marked by dancing **monks** and candlelit gatherings under the full moon.

The Sherpas of Nepal

Did you know?
Sherpas often perform better than other climbers because they have lived in the thin mountain air all their lives. They are so well-known for their skills that all native Himalayan guides are now called Sherpas.

The Sherpa people live high in the Himalayas. Following an ancient form of Buddhism, they believe their mountains are the homes of gods. The steep slopes are strung with prayer flags and decorated with carved *mani* stones. Prayer wheels spin in the wind. Cars and bicycles are nowhere to be found in Sherpa villages. Sherpas walk or climb everywhere.

Once, nearly all Sherpas grew potatoes or herded yaks. Today, many have become **porters** and guides for mountain climbers. Sherpas can work and climb easily in the mountain air. Many have a goal of reaching the summit of Everest. Sherpa traditions add to the richness and beauty of the Himalayas and all of Nepal.

fun fact

A Sherpa called Tenzing Norgay was one of the first two men to reach the top of Everest. He climbed the mountain with New Zealander Sir Edmund Hillary in 1953.

Fast Facts About Nepal

Nepal's Flag

Nepal's flag is shaped like two overlapping triangles. It is the only flag in the world that is not a rectangle. The triangles are bright red with a blue border. The top triangle shows a white moon. The bottom triangle features a white sun. The colors stand for bravery and peace. The sun and moon are symbols of long life. The current flag first flew in 1962.

Official Name: Federal Democratic Republic of Nepal

Area: 56,827 square miles (147,181 square kilometers); Nepal is the 94th largest country in the world.

Capital City:	Kathmandu
Important Cities:	Pokhara, Patan, Biratnagar
Population:	30,430,267 (July 2013)
Official Language:	Nepali
National Holiday:	Republic Day (May 29)
Religions:	Hindu (80.6%), Buddhist (10.7%), Muslim (4.2%), Kirant (3.6%), other (0.9%)
Major Industries:	farming, tourism
Natural Resources:	timber, coal, copper, iron ore, limestone
Manufactured Products:	food products, building materials, clothing, carpets
Farm Products:	rice, corn, wheat, sugarcane, potatoes, jute, milk, water buffalo
Unit of Money:	Nepalese rupee; the rupee is divided into 100 paise.

Glossary

ancestors—relatives who lived long ago

avalanches—large masses of snow or ice that suddenly break away from and slide down the sides of mountains

caste—one of the social classes in Hinduism that people are born into and that governs their behavior and life decisions

chariots—small vehicles pulled by horses or other means

crevasses—large, deep cracks in the earth or in glaciers

endangered—at risk of becoming extinct

fertile—able to support growth

glaciers—massive sheets of ice that cover large areas of land

landlocked—completely surrounded by land

marshes—areas of soft, wet land often covered in grasses

monks—men who live apart from society in religious communities called monasteries; monks often live according to strict religious rules.

native—originally from a specific place

porters—people who carry supplies and equipment for others

service jobs—jobs that perform tasks for people or businesses

shrines—places, buildings, or objects that are considered holy

summit—the highest point of something

terraced—carved into a series of flat areas or steps of land; hills and mountains are often terraced so people can grow farms on flat land.

tourists—people who travel to visit another place

traditional—relating to a custom, idea, or belief handed down from one generation to the next

yak—a type of shaggy ox that lives in and around Tibet; yaks do well in the mountains and are often used to carry loads.

To Learn More

AT THE LIBRARY
Burleigh, Robert. *Tiger of the Snows: Tenzing Norgay: The Boy Whose Dream Was Everest*. New York, N.Y.: Atheneum Books for Young Readers, 2006.

Rosinsky, Natalie M. *Hinduism*. Minneapolis, Minn.: Compass Point Books, 2009.

Spilsbury, Louise. *Living in the Himalaya*. Chicago, Ill.: Raintree, 2008.

ON THE WEB
Learning more about Nepal is as easy as 1, 2, 3.

1. Go to www.factsurfer.com.

2. Enter "Nepal" into the search box.

3. Click the "Surf" button and you will see a list of related Web sites.

With factsurfer.com, finding more information is just a click away.

Index

activities, 9, 20, 21
Bisket Jatra, 25
capital (see Kathmandu)
climate, 6, 7, 9
daily life, 14-15
Dashain, 24
education, 16-17
food, 22-23
Himalayas, 4, 5, 6, 7, 14, 23, 26, 27
Holi, 25
holidays, 24-25
housing, 14, 15
Kathmandu, 5, 15, 19
landscape, 6-9
language, 12, 13, 17
location, 4-5
Mount Everest, 8-9, 27
Norgay, Tenzing, 27
peoples, 12-13, 26-27
religion, 12, 13, 15, 23, 24, 25, 27
Republic Day, 24
Sherpas, 9, 26-27
sports, 20
Tihar, 24
transportation, 14, 15, 27
wildlife, 10-11
working, 13, 14, 17, 18-19, 27
yeti, 9

The images in this book are reproduced through the courtesy of: Vixit, front cover, pp. 8-9; Martin M303, pp. 6-7; Volodymyr Goinyk, p. 7; Minden Pictures/ SuperStock, pp. 10-11; Atthapol Saita, p. 11 (top); Hung Chung Chih, pp. 11 (middle), 15; Victortyakht, p. 11 (bottom); Paper Boat Creative/ Getty Images, p. 12; Jiri Foltyn, p. 14; Bruno Morandi/ Getty Images, pp. 16-17; Bruce Yeung, p. 18; hadynyah, pp. 19 (left & right), 26-27; Jane Sweeney/ Getty Images, p. 20; Biosphoto/ SuperStock, p. 21; Ahmad Faizal Yahya, p. 22; percom, p. 23 (left); Photocuisine/ SuperStock, p. 23 (right); Prakash Mathema/ Stringer/ AFP/ Getty Images/ Newscom, pp. 24, 25 (left); Narendra Shrestha/ EPA/ Newscom, p. 25 (right); Maisei Raman, p. 28; Jason Maehl, p. 29.